**CORNERSTONES OF FREEDOM™**

# THE U.S. CONSTITUTION

## BY MICHAEL BURGAN

**CHILDREN'S PRESS®**
An Imprint of Scholastic Inc.
New York  Toronto  London  Auckland  Sydney
Mexico City  New Delhi  Hong Kong
Danbury, Connecticut

Content Consultant:
Rogers Smith, PhD
Christopher H. Brown
Distinguished Professor of
Political Science
University of Pennsylvania
Philadelphia, Pennsylvania

Library of Congress Cataloging-in-Publication Data

Burgan, Michael.
  The U.S. Constitution/by Michael Burgan.
    p. cm.—(Cornerstones of freedom)
  Includes bibliographical references and index.
  ISBN-13: 978-0-531-25042-6 (lib. bdg.)     ISBN-10: 0-531-25042-3 (lib. bdg.)
  ISBN-13: 978-0-531-26567-3 (pbk.)          ISBN-10: 0-531-26567-6 (pbk.)
  1. United States. Constitution—Juvenile literature. 2.
Constitutional history—United States—Juvenile literature. 3. United
States—Politics and government—1775–1783—Juvenile literature.
4. United States—Politics and government—1783–1789—Juvenile
literature.
  I. Title.
  E303.B884 2011
  342.7302′9—dc22                            2011011309

All rights reserved. Published in 2012 by Children's Press, an imprint of
Scholastic Inc.
Printed in the United States of America 113
SCHOLASTIC, CHILDREN'S PRESS, CORNERSTONES OF FREEDOM™,
and associated logos are trademarks and/or registered trademarks of
Scholastic Inc.

1 2 3 4 5 6 7 8 9 10 R 21 20 19 18 17 16 15 14 13 12

Photographs © 2012: Alamy Images/Michael Ventura: 54; AP Images:
42 (Pablo Martinez Monsivais), 4 bottom, 6, 8, 15 bottom, 22, 27, 32, 33,
36, 43, 45, 47, 56 bottom (North Wind Picture Archives); Architect of the
Capitol, Washington, DC/John Trumbull: back cover; Getty Images/MPI/
Stringer: 37; iStockphoto: cover (Sean Locke), 5 bottom, 28 (Lee Pettet);
Library of Congress: 20 (Constantino Brumidi/Detroit Publishing Co.), 5 top,
15 top, 56 top (Joseph-Siffrède Duplessis), 46, 58 (Sherwood Lithograph
Co.), 21, 57 (Gilbert Stuart), 16 (Gilbert Stuart/Detroit Publishing Co.), 13
(John Trumbull/Detroit Publishing Co.); Michael Burgan: 64; National
Archives and Records Administration: 38; North Wind Picture Archives:
25; Superstock, Inc.: 35 (Hy Hintermeister), 14 (J.B. Longacre/Universal
Images Group), 44 (Rembrandt Peale), 30 (Peter Frederick Rothermel), 12
(Gilbert Stuart/Universal Images Group), 18, 49; The Granger Collection,
New York: 26 (George Catlin), 11, 34, 48, 59; The Image Works: 2, 3, 40 (Rob
Crandall), 4 top, 50 (Charles Gatewood), 24 (Roger-Viollet), 10 (Topham), 23
(World History Archive/Topfoto), 17.

BRINGING
HISTORY
to LIFE

# Did you know that studying history can be fun?

**BRING HISTORY TO LIFE** by becoming a history investigator. Examine the evidence (primary and secondary source materials); cross-examine the people and witnesses. Take a look at what was happening at the time—but be careful! What happened years ago might suddenly become incredibly interesting and change the way you think!

# Contents

# Independence— and Problems

**George Washington's victory at Yorktown ended the last major battle between British and American soldiers during the American Revolution.**

Many American soldiers whooped with joy on the battlefield at Yorktown, Virginia. Their defeated foes tossed their guns on a heap. It was October 19, 1781. British forces had surrendered to General George Washington, leader of America's Continental army.

This victory brought the major fighting of the American Revolutionary War to a close. The colonies were free from British rule.

The 13 original colonies had formed a national government for their new nation even before their victory. A document called the Articles of Confederation spelled out the powers of Congress. Congress is the branch of government that makes laws. The articles also described the rights and duties of the individual states. Some Americans thought the Articles of Confederation had not created the best government possible.

Alexander Hamilton from New York wanted Americans to have a strong national government. Hamilton thought the government also needed an **executive** who was separate from Congress. The executive and the departments under him would have the power to enforce laws. Hamilton also wanted a national government that could settle disputes between states and make them pay the taxes they owed. Under the Articles of Confederation, Congress could not force the states to pay taxes.

Concerns about the Articles of Confederation grew. Important American political leaders met in Philadelphia, Pennsylvania, in 1787 to improve the articles. They ended up creating a new form of government. It resulted in a document called the U.S. Constitution. That government still works today to protect the rights and freedoms of all Americans.

# CHAPTER 1

# TIME FOR A CHANGE

Daniel Shays led protests against high taxes in Massachusetts.

# Daniel Shays was angry.

The farmer from western Massachusetts had fought the British for America's freedom and independence. Now he thought his own state government was treating him unfairly.

Massachusetts had raised its taxes in the years after the revolution to pay for war expenses. The state wanted residents to pay the new taxes with metal coins. Coins then had more value than paper money. But farmers such as Shays and his neighbors usually did not receive coins for the crops they sold. They traded for other goods or received paper money.

**Shays's Rebellion was waged mostly by small farmers who were angered by taxes and deeply in debt.**

By 1786, Shays and others asked the state government to help them. Instead, farmers who were in **debt** were forced to go to court. Mobs of protesters began shutting down the courts that decided whether or not debtors would go to jail. Shays helped shut down one court. He was a leader in a movement called Shays's Rebellion by the end of the year. In early 1787, Massachusetts troops and Shays's small band of protesters clashed several times.

## Seeking a Solution

The problems in Massachusetts drew national attention. Congress asked the states to raise money so it could send troops to Massachusetts to end the protests. Only Virginia agreed. This highlighted a weakness in the Articles of Confederation. Congress could not force the other states to raise money.

News of Shays's Rebellion reached General George Washington. He feared the new nation might break apart if protests spread. Washington disliked Congress and its weak powers even before the events in Massachusetts. He called Congress "a half-starved, limping government, that appears to be always moving upon crutches and tottering at every step."

### SPOTLIGHT ON

### The Annapolis Convention

Virginia's lawmakers called for the first meeting to discuss changing the Articles of Confederation. It was held in Annapolis, Maryland, in September 1786 and was called the Annapolis Convention. Only **delegates** from Delaware, New Jersey, New York, Pennsylvania, and Virginia attended. Some other states sent delegates, but they did not arrive in time. Several states chose not to participate at all. Alexander Hamilton and Virginia's James Madison led the effort in Annapolis to ask Congress to change the articles. Madison would later play the key role in writing the Constitution. He and Hamilton worked together to make sure Americans would accept it.

Others who shared that view had already tried to take action. In September 1786, lawmakers from several states met to discuss changing the Articles of Confederation. They sent their suggestion to Congress. Congress agreed in February 1787 that the states should hold a convention in Philadelphia, Pennsylvania. Several men from each state, called delegates, would meet to discuss the articles. Shays's Rebellion was just about over by this time. But political disagreements in other states had convinced more people that the country had to create a stronger national government.

**James Madison was one of the major figures of early U.S. government.**

**Alexander Hamilton believed the new nation needed a strong central government.**

## The Convention Begins

Delegates from the states began arriving in Philadelphia in May 1787. Like Madison and Hamilton, others were already thinking about what they wanted to do. Making **amendments** to the Articles of Confederation was not enough. The country needed an entirely new government that would be split into three branches. The **legislative** branch was called Congress. It would make laws. The executive branch would carry out the laws. A

**Delegate Robert Morris later became one of the first two senators from Pennsylvania.**

separate **judicial** branch would make sure the laws were fairly enforced. Sharing the power would mean no one branch could completely control the government. Most of the states already had similar forms of government. The new government would share **sovereignty** with the individual states. All power would ultimately remain with the people. Some of it would stay assigned to the states. The new national government would have broad powers to use for the good of all the people of the United States.

The delegates who came to Philadelphia included some of the country's best thinkers. Benjamin Franklin was a scientist and a student of government. Robert Morris had provided money for Washington's army. Others had written articles defending American rights against the British. More than half had fought in the war or served in

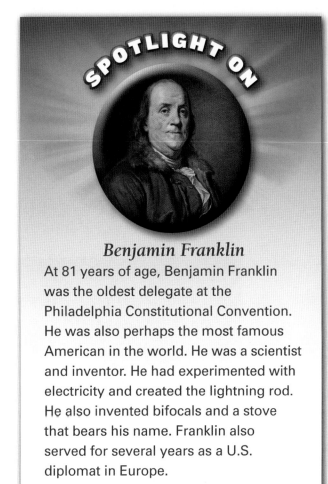

*Benjamin Franklin*
At 81 years of age, Benjamin Franklin was the oldest delegate at the Philadelphia Constitutional Convention. He was also perhaps the most famous American in the world. He was a scientist and inventor. He had experimented with electricity and created the lightning rod. He also invented bifocals and a stove that bears his name. Franklin also served for several years as a U.S. diplomat in Europe.

**Benjamin Franklin (at table, left), Alexander Hamilton (at table, right), and others at the Constitutional Convention discuss the new government.**

Congress. Many were wealthy, though some had risen from simple backgrounds and worked hard.

The most respected delegate at the convention was George Washington. Washington did not try to gain political power after leading the Americans to victory against the British. He simply returned to his farm in

**George Washington led the colonial army in America's fight against the British.**

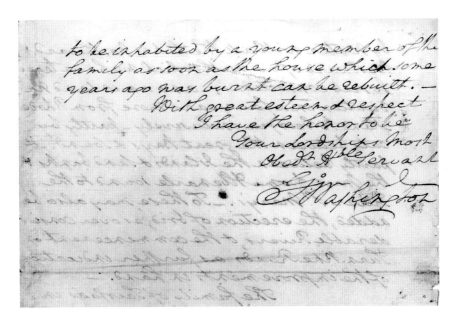

**In a 1793 letter to a friend in England, Washington wrote about plans for a new city, which would later become Washington, D.C.**

Virginia. The delegates all voted for Washington when they met to choose someone to lead the convention. Delegates from several states had still not arrived by the end of May. The convention's work began anyway.

## A FIRSTHAND LOOK AT
## GEORGE WASHINGTON'S DIARIES

George Washington wrote 51 diaries that kept track of the people he met and what he did. Washington referred to them simply as "Where & How my Time is Spent." The diaries begin in 1748 and continue through 1799. They contain notes about his stay in Philadelphia. They are kept at the Library of Congress in Washington, D.C. See page 60 for a link to view the original diaries.

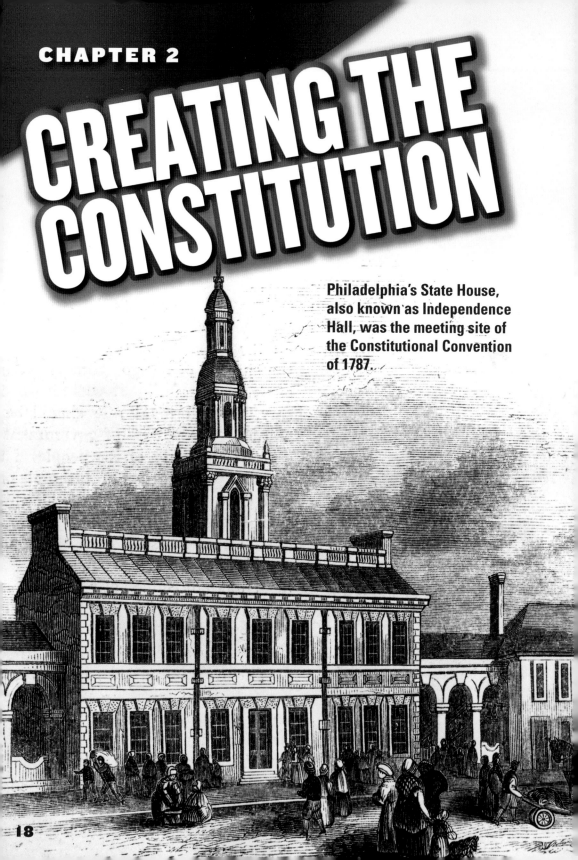

# CHAPTER 2

# CREATING THE CONSTITUTION

Philadelphia's State House, also known as Independence Hall, was the meeting site of the Constitutional Convention of 1787.

ON TUESDAY, MAY 29, 1787, delegates from nine states gathered in Philadelphia's State House. They were ready to start their convention. Delegates would soon arrive from three more states. Only Rhode Island chose not to send anyone. Some of its lawmakers liked the Articles of Confederation. George Washington later wrote that it was "unjust" and "scandalous" for the state to ignore the convention.

**At the convention, Edmund Randolph argued for a strong central government and the establishment of a three-branch government.**

Edmund Randolph of Virginia addressed the delegates. He said the articles should be "corrected and enlarged" to guarantee the "common defense, security of liberty and general welfare" of all Americans. Then he proposed a plan for a new **federal** government that would balance powers between a stronger central government and the states.

Randolph had help developing his plan. Virginia delegates had previously met to lay out the details of what came to be called the Virginia Plan. But James Madison has often been seen as the driving force behind the plan. The plan drew on European thinking and the systems of government already at work in most of the states.

## Debating the Virginia Plan

The Virginia Plan called for the three-branch government made up of a legislature, an executive, and a judicial system. The legislature would be divided into two houses. Citizens would elect the lawmakers of the "lower" house. Those lawmakers would choose the members of the "upper" house. The legislature would address national issues and have the power to overturn state laws that conflicted with the national interest.

### James Madison

James Madison's sharp intelligence and writing skills helped make him one of America's greatest political thinkers. Bad health kept him out of the Revolutionary War. But Madison served in the Virginia government before representing his home state in Congress. He became famous for his work on the Constitution and later the Bill of Rights. Madison also kept a journal that is one of the best records of what was said at the Philadelphia Constitutional Convention. In 1808, he was elected the fourth president of the United States and served for eight years.

The plan called for the executive and members of the judiciary to form a council that would review the laws passed by the national legislature.

Within two days, the delegates voted to accept a national government with three distinct branches and a legislature with two houses. But for the next two months they often disagreed on the details of how the government would work. Delegates from larger states wanted each state to elect lawmakers based on its population. Delegates from the smaller states opposed this. The convention also considered how a state's population would be counted. Southern states with many slaves wanted each slave to be counted as one person. Northern states opposed this. They had much smaller slave populations.

Some small states wanted to keep the basic structure of the Articles of Confederation and make minor changes. They presented their ideas in what was called the New Jersey Plan. But the Virginia Plan remained the main source of ideas for the new government.

**Delegates at the convention debated many important issues, such as how each state would be represented in Congress.**

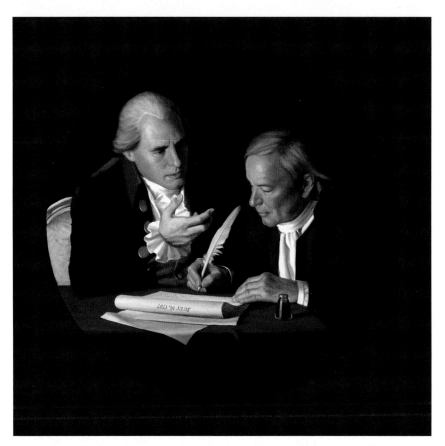

**Delegates Roger Sherman (right) and Oliver Ellsworth (left) of Connecticut resolved the issue of state representation by creating the Great Compromise.**

The issue of how the national legislature would work was finally settled with the Great (or Connecticut) **Compromise**. It said that the number of representatives each state sent to the lower house would be based on its population. Larger states would get more representatives than smaller ones. Each slave would count as three-fifths of a person for this purpose. Each state would have the same number of representatives as all the other states in the upper house.

Many delegates feared the powers that Madison and others wanted to give the new national government.

Delegates such as Luther Martin of Maryland and Robert Yates of New York expressed this concern. These supporters of states' rights won a victory when the convention decided not to create a national Council of Revision that could overturn state laws. But Madison and his supporters saw most of their ideas accepted as the convention went on.

**The Great Compromise determined that each slave would be counted as three-fifths of a person for representation purposes.**

In December 1790, the nation's capital was moved from New York City to Philadelphia (above).

## Other Issues

The delegates debated the basic format of the new government into July. Then, from July 26 until August 6, a smaller committee summed up much of what had already been discussed. The committee also added new details. The full convention then met to discuss this first draft of what would become the Constitution.

This draft called the legislative branch Congress—as the Articles of Confederation had done—and named its two branches. The lower house would be the House of Representatives. The upper house would be the Senate. The leader of the executive branch would be called the president. The draft also gave Congress specific power

**Each delegate carefully explained his ideas to the others.**

to collect several kinds of taxes and to have control over
**commerce** between the states. Under the draft, members
of Congress would elect the president. The president
could serve only one seven-year term.

Some delegates wanted the people to play a more
direct role in electing the president. This led to a system
called the Electoral College. Each state would name
electors. These electors would choose the president,
usually based on whom the voters in their state
preferred. The number of electors each state had was the
same as the number of lawmakers it sent to Congress.
The delegates also decided that Congress could remove
from office a president who broke the law. Finally, the
delegates set a president's term at four years. They did

not place limits on how many terms could be served.

The debates over the committee's draft went on for five weeks. Many of the delegates had been away from home for several months by this time. Some had left the convention and then returned. Others left and did not come back. Those who stayed were eager to make compromises and agreements so they could finish their work.

But slavery was one issue that stirred strong feelings. Delegates argued whether the government should be able to tax the slave trade. Others wanted

The delegates agreed not to discuss with the public what went on at the convention during the debates. But rumors began to spread that the new government might have a king. A Pennsylvania newspaper published a comment from an unnamed delegate who said, "We are well informed, that many letters have been written to the members of the federal convention … that it is intended to establish a monarchical government … though we cannot, affirmatively, tell you what we are doing, we can, negatively, tell you what we are not doing—we never once thought of a king."

to totally stop the buying of slaves from overseas. The delegates eventually placed limits on how many taxes could be collected on the slave trade. If Congress wanted, the overseas slave trade would end in 1808. Yet the words slave and slavery never appeared in the final version of the Constitution. This hinted at how divided some Americans already were over slavery.

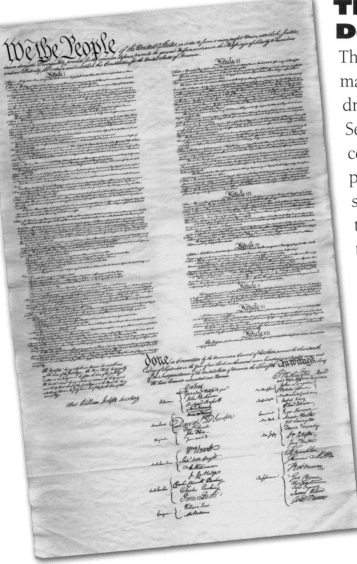

The final Constitution provided a blueprint for the new government.

## The Final Document

The delegates finished making changes to the draft document on September 8. Another committee met to polish the writing style. A few days later, the delegates made their last minor changes. They also discussed including a bill of rights, a list of specific rights that the new national government could never take away. Several states had bills of rights in their constitutions. They guaranteed such things as free speech and the freedom to follow any religion. The Philadelphia delegates rejected a bill of rights for the new Constitution. Agreeing to the details of a bill could take weeks. The delegates were ready to go home now.

Most of the remaining 41 delegates finally signed the Constitution on September 17. Three who did not approve of the document did not sign. Writing to his father, New Hampshire delegate Nicholas Gilman, who did sign it, noted how often the delegates had compromised. The final document was not perfect. But Gilman believed that forming a new government based on the Constitution would decide if the United States "shall become a respectable nation, or a people torn to pieces by . . . commotions."

Now, the decision to **ratify** the Constitution would be decided by American voters.

## A FIRSTHAND LOOK AT
## THE PREAMBLE

A preamble is the opening part of an important document. The preamble for the Constitution was written by Gouverneur Morris of New Jersey. Morris wrote that the new government was meant to "secure the blessings of liberty" of Americans then and in the future. The original copy of the Constitution is kept on public display at the National Archives in Washington, D.C. See page 60 for a link to view the document.

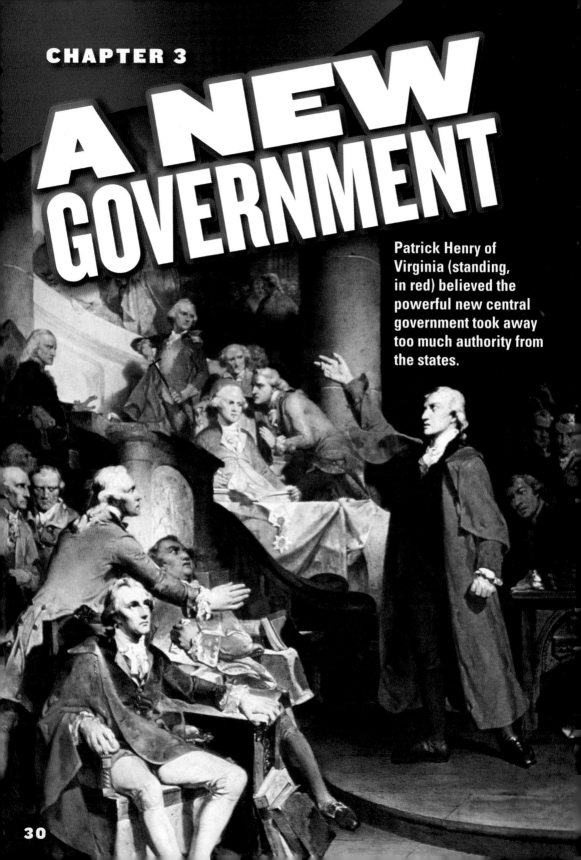

# CHAPTER 3

# A NEW GOVERNMENT

Patrick Henry of Virginia (standing, in red) believed the powerful new central government took away too much authority from the states.

EACH STATE NOW HAD TO VOTE whether or not to accept the Constitution. Nine states had to ratify the document for it to take effect. Each state would hold its own convention. The delegates would be elected by the voters. These delegates would decide if their state ratified the Constitution.

**Shipping was an important business in colonial America. The counting house of a shipping business was where financial transactions were conducted.**

In December 1787, Delaware became the first state to ratify the Constitution. Every delegate at its convention voted to approve it. New Jersey and Georgia also voted **unanimously** to ratify it. But the process slowed a bit when delegates in some states strongly opposed the new government outlined in the Constitution. They were called anti-Federalists. Americans who supported the Constitution, such as Benjamin Franklin and George Washington, were called Federalists.

The anti-Federalists thought the new government took too much power from the states. Many, including Patrick Henry of Virginia, argued this. In June 1788, he said, "Liberty ought to be the direct end of your government." But he thought that freedom was threatened without a guarantee of such things as free speech and the right to a trial by a jury.

Federalists James Madison and Alexander Hamilton were hard at work trying to convince delegates to support the Constitution. Along with John Jay of New York, they wrote a series of newspaper articles defending the new government. The articles were later published in a book called *The Federalist Papers*.

Hamilton told his readers in the first article that ratifying the Constitution was "the safest course for your liberty, your dignity, and your happiness." The new,

## SPOTLIGHT ON

### Patrick Henry

As a young lawyer from Virginia, Patrick Henry had strongly opposed British efforts to tax the colonies. He attacked King George III in some of his speeches. This upset lawmakers who supported the king. Henry apologized for some of his harsh remarks. But he became famous for speaking his mind. In March 1775, as the Revolutionary War approached, he famously cried, "Give me liberty, or give me death." He served as governor of Virginia several times.

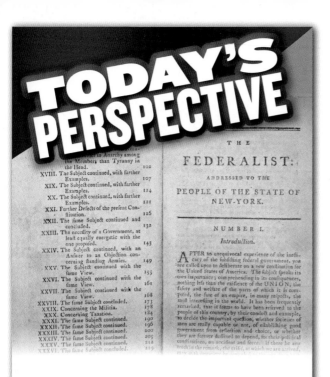

# TODAY'S PERSPECTIVE

None of the authors of the original *Federalist* articles signed their names. Instead, they all used the false name of Publius. Political writers of the 18th century often chose to hide their true identities so they could speak freely. Modern scholars believe that Hamilton wrote more than half of the 85 articles. Jay probably wrote only five. The original articles did not have a wide impact across America. But today, *The Federalist* is considered one of the country's most important political documents.

stronger government would make it easier for the country to defend itself from foreign attack and to increase its wealth.

## The Bill of Rights

New Hampshire became the ninth state to ratify the Constitution on June 21, 1788. The new government would take effect. But many political leaders closely watched the debates in New York and Virginia. They were among the largest and wealthiest states. The strength of the new government might be threatened if they voted against the Constitution. The vote in both states was close, but the Federalists won. Delegates in both states called for amendments to the Constitution. Virginia joined several other states in asking for a bill of rights. North Carolina

**George Washington was sworn in as the nation's first president at Federal Hall in New York City.**

and Rhode Island did not ratify the Constitution. They remained out of the **Union** for a time.

The Constitution was approved. The country prepared to elect a new Congress and its first president. The choice for president was unanimous. George Washington was the best person to lead the new government. He was sworn in as president on April 30, 1789. He promised to "preserve, protect and defend the Constitution of the United States."

**Federal Hall in New York City served as a meetinghouse for colonists before the Revolutionary War and was later the first capitol building of the United States.**

The new government met in New York City, which was then serving as the nation's capital. Congress soon began considering its first laws. James Madison was a member of the House of Representatives. His job was to write a bill of rights for Congress to consider. The bill would go to the states for ratification once lawmakers approved it.

But some lawmakers thought Congress had more important issues to address first. It had to create executive departments to help the president and work out the details of the judicial system. Some Federalists believed that the people had accepted the Constitution as it was so there was no need to change it. Some anti-Federalists were not actually as interested in a bill of rights as they once claimed. What they really wanted was a new constitutional convention. They wanted to change the new government in major ways.

Madison wanted to balance the interests of Federalists and anti-Federalists. He wrote that he hoped to "satisfy the public mind that their liberties will be perpetual [permanent] . . . without endangering any part of the constitution."

Madison drafted many proposed amendments. They included freedom of speech and of the press; freedom of religion; and the right to own guns. One also said

**The painting *Signing the Constitution of the United States* by Thomas Prichard Rossiter shows the delegates approving the document that would govern the nation.**

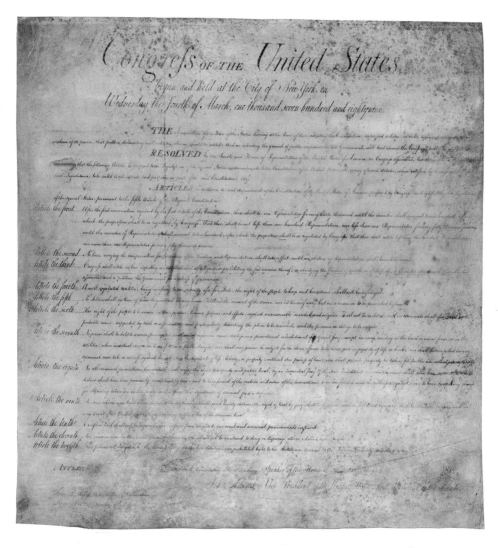

**The Bill of Rights guaranteed many personal freedoms not specifically spelled out in the original version of the Constitution.**

that any power not granted to the new government, or denied to the states, belonged to the states and the people. Anti-Federalists believed this was a good check on the power of the federal government.

# A FIRSTHAND LOOK AT
## THE BILL OF RIGHTS

Congress has kept a written record of its activities since 1789. The document outlining the first 12 proposed amendments to the Constitution is on display at the National Archives in Washington, D.C. See page 60 for a link to view the original document.

In August 1789, the House agreed on most of the amendments and sent them to the Senate. It finally approved 12 of them. The legislatures of each state then debated whether to ratify the amendments. Under the Constitution, three-fourths of the states had to approve an amendment for it to take effect. By 1791, enough states approved 10 of the amendments. They were then added to the Constitution as the Bill of Rights. The Bill of Rights helped convince North Carolina and Rhode Island to finally join the Union.

Most Americans seemed satisfied with their new government after the ratification of the Bill of Rights. President Washington and the new Congress focused on running the country. But the Constitution continued to shape the United States.

# CHAPTER 4

# A LIVING DOCUMENT

Both houses of Congress join together to listen to the president's State of the Union address each year.

THOUSANDS OF NEW AMENDMENTS to the Constitution have been proposed since 1791. Few have actually been approved. Amendments make the Constitution what some people call a "living" document.

The Constitution is also alive in the sense that the U.S. Supreme Court has interpreted the government's powers more broadly at certain times. The court can use a process called judicial review to decide if federal and state laws are **constitutional**.

**The Supreme Court is composed of nine justices who are appointed for life.**

## New Amendments

The Constitution called for a federal court system made of one supreme court and any other courts Congress chose to create. The federal courts would look at legal issues that related to the Constitution itself, federal laws, and foreign affairs. The federal courts would also handle conflicts between two states, between citizens of two states, and between the citizen of one state and the government of another.

The first amendment after the Bill of Rights resulted from a U.S. Supreme Court decision. The court said that a private citizen from South Carolina could sue the state of Georgia. Georgia argued that the resident of another state could not sue it in a federal court. Anti-Federalists wanted similar cases in the future to be decided in state courts. They did not want the federal government to have a legal say in disputes that did not directly involve federal law. The anti-Federalists got their way in 1794 with the 11th Amendment to the Constitution. It spelled out this limit on the federal courts to hear disputes between the government of one state and the citizen of another, if no federal law was involved.

The next amendment also came in response to one specific event. The presidential election of 1800 pitted Thomas Jefferson against John Adams, Aaron Burr, and two other men. Jefferson and Burr received the same number of electoral votes. This tie meant the House of

**The U.S. Supreme Court hears the nation's most important cases.**

**Thomas Jefferson ran against John Adams for president in 1800.**

Representatives would choose the winner. The vote in the House dragged on for almost a week. Neither man could win enough votes. Jefferson finally won.

## A FIRSTHAND LOOK AT
## A VICTORY BANNER

The Constitution did not mention political parties. But they emerged on their own during the 1790s. John Adams ran for the Federalists in the 1800 presidential election. Thomas Jefferson was the head of a new party called the Democratic Republicans. Jefferson's victory was celebrated on a cloth banner. The banner is kept at the Smithsonian Institution in Washington, D.C. See page 60 for a link to view the banner.

Part of the problem with the election came from the Constitution itself. The electors in the Electoral College did not vote separately for president and vice president. Jefferson and Burr were from the same political party. The party's electoral voters simply split their votes between the two men. This created a tie. Congress proposed the 12th Amendment in 1804 to prevent this from happening again. It required the Electoral College to vote separately for a president and vice president.

## The Civil War Amendments

The 11th and 12th amendments sprang from reactions to specific legal issues. Amendments 13 through 15 dealt with slavery. Slavery was almost ignored in the original Constitution. The three amendments came at the end of the Civil War.

**Slavery became a controversial issue in the years leading up to the Civil War.**

Abraham Lincoln was elected president in 1860. He had promised to try to stop the spread of slavery into new states and territories. But he also said he would not seek to end slavery in the states where it already existed. Slavery was allowed under the Constitution. But a number of states outlawed it in the years after the Constitution was ratified. By 1860, most of the remaining slave states were in the South. They feared any efforts by the federal government to end slavery.

Lawmakers in the slave states believed that laws against slavery were unconstitutional. They knew Lincoln supported a ban of slavery in America's western territories. They feared he would not keep his promise to allow slavery where it already existed. Wishing to maintain slaves, South Carolina seceded, or left, the Union. Other Southern states followed. Lincoln said

**President Lincoln was against the spread of slavery.**

**The passing of the 13th Amendment, abolishing slavery, inspired celebration in the House of Representatives.**

that these states had no right under the Constitution to secede. He was prepared to fight to protect federal property in the Southern states and to keep the Union together.

Many other Americans believed that the American Civil War was originally fought over what the Constitution did or did not allow. But Lincoln and others saw as the war went on that the result of the fighting would decide if slavery would last in the United States. The North's victory guaranteed that slavery would end.

The 13th Amendment outlawed slavery forever. The 14th Amendment stated that anyone born in the United States and subject to its jurisdiction was a U.S. citizen. Most slaves at the time had been born in the country. They received the rights of U.S. citizens. They were also

**Women in New York City marched to celebrate passage of the 19th Amendment, which gave them voting rights.**

considered citizens of the states where they lived. The 15th Amendment granted to African American men the right to vote.

One particular part of the 14th Amendment had even broader effects on the rights of all Americans. It said states could not pass laws that denied anyone "equal protection" or "life, liberty, or property without due process of law." One effect of this, the U.S. Supreme Court later ruled, was that the Bill of Rights applied to state governments as well as the federal government. A state law that tried to limit free speech could be challenged in federal courts. The court also found that certain rights not specifically mentioned in the Bill of Rights were also protected. Perhaps the most important was a right to privacy. This right was announced by the court in 1965.

## The Next 12 Amendments

The 15th Amendment was ratified in 1870. Only 12 more have been added to the Constitution since then. The 17th Amendment was ratified in 1913. It gave voters the right to directly elect their U.S. senators. The Constitution originally gave that right to the lawmakers in each state. The 19th Amendment gave women the right to vote. When it was ratified in 1920, some states had already given women this right. But the amendment made it the law of the land.

Several amendments to the Constitution have limited people's rights. In 1919, the

# YESTERDAY'S HEADLINES

President Richard Nixon invited a group of young Americans to the White House to watch the ceremony that officially made the 26th Amendment part of the Constitution.

"I sense that we can have confidence that America's new voters, America's young generation, will provide what America needs as we approach our two hundredth birthday, not just strength and not just wealth but the 'Spirit of '76,' a spirit of moral courage, a spirit of high idealism in which we believe in the American dream, but in which we realize that the American dream can never be fulfilled until every American has an equal chance to fulfill it in his own life," President Nixon said.

**The Equal Rights Amendment was a proposed amendment to the Constitution saying that equal rights could not be denied on the basis of sex. The amendment has never been passed.**

18th Amendment made it illegal for Americans to make or sell alcohol if it was used as a drink. This amendment was overturned in 1933 with the 21st Amendment. This newer amendment made alcohol legal again unless states chose to ban it. The 22nd Amendment states that a president can serve only two terms.

Two more amendments dealt with voting rights. The 24th Amendment was ratified in 1964. It said states could not charge a poll tax. This tax was charged to all people who wanted to vote. Many southern states had poll taxes to try to keep African Americans from voting. Many African Americans were poor and could not afford the tax. Seven years later, the 26th Amendment lowered the voting age across the country from 21 to 18.

As of 2012, the last amendment to the Constitution was actually an old one. The 27th Amendment, ratified in 1992, was the same as one that the states had rejected when first considering the Bill of Rights. This latest amendment limits when Congress can grant itself pay raises.

The Constitution continues to address both the details of the U.S. government and the greater issues of freedoms and rights.

# A VIEW FROM ABROAD

Charles-Louis de Secondat, Baron de Montesquieu (1689–1755) was a French philosopher. He argued the need for a separation of powers within a government in his book *The Spirit of the Laws*, published in 1748. James Madison was heavily influenced by Montesquieu's belief that the best way to secure liberty and guarantee freedoms was to divide the powers of government among branches that would check each other. Montesquieu warned that an all-powerful executive power with no check on its authority would soon destroy all the other powers. Madison and the other creators of the Constitution agreed, and subsequently created the three branches of government in use today.

# What Happened Where?

**Philadelphia** was the site of the signing of the Declaration of Independence in 1776 as well as the Constitutional Convention of 1787. It also served as the U.S. capital from 1790 to 1800.

**Washington, D.C.,** was chosen as the site for the permanent U.S capital. The Constitution called for selecting such a site. Maryland and Virginia donated the land for it.

GA

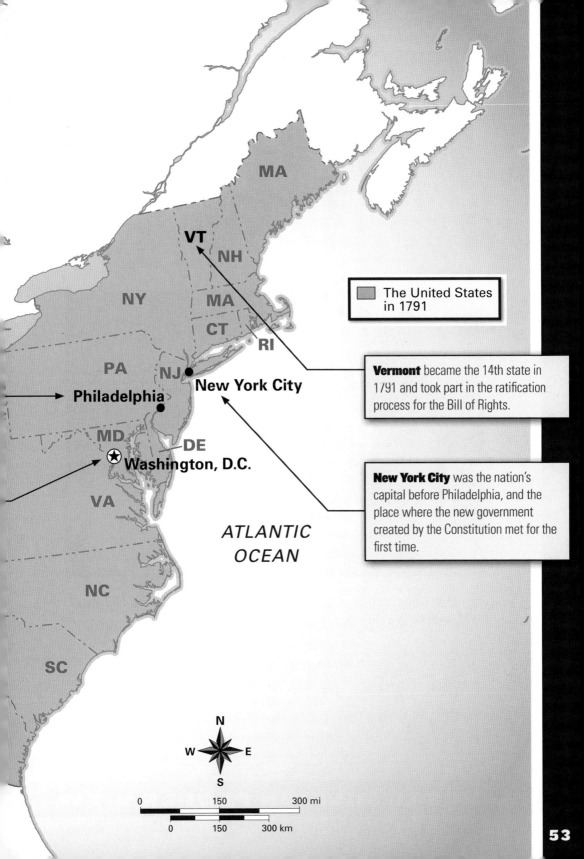

MA

VT

NH

NY

MA

CT

RI

PA

NJ •

**New York City**

**Philadelphia**
•

MD

DE

⊛ **Washington, D.C.**

VA

NC

SC

ATLANTIC
OCEAN

The United States
in 1791

**Vermont** became the 14th state in
1/91 and took part in the ratification
process for the Bill of Rights.

**New York City** was the nation's
capital before Philadelphia, and the
place where the new government
created by the Constitution met for the
first time.

N
W — E
S

| 0 | 150 | 300 mi |

| 0 | 150 | 300 km |

# The Constitution Today

**The U.S. Constitution is on display in the Rotunda of the National Archives in Washington, D.C.**

Members of Congress spend time considering the Constitution. Each year some of them propose new amendments. Some recent proposals have called for eliminating the Electoral College and letting voters directly choose the president. Another would allow U.S. citizens born outside the United States to become president, after they have lived in the country for a certain number of years. The Constitution currently only allows people born in the country to hold that office.

The Supreme Court continues to decide if state and federal laws follow the Constitution or not. Some justices try to follow exactly what they think the country's founders meant and what they said in the years after. Other justices think it's impossible to know what the founders would have thought about such modern problems as terrorism and privacy on the Internet.

Some Americans think the time has come for a new constitutional convention. The Constitution itself describes the process for calling such a convention. Legislatures in two-thirds of the states must support the convention. Then any proposed amendments that emerge must be passed by three-quarters of the states. Some people who support a new convention think it should only address specific issues. But opponents fear the topics could not be limited. They fear the changes to the Constitution that might emerge from such a convention.

Whatever problems the current U.S. government has, most people believe the Constitution created a system that helps balance the freedoms of Americans with the needs of the states and the federal government.

# INFLUENTIAL INDIVIDUALS

Benjamin Franklin

**Benjamin Franklin** (1706–1790) began his career as a printer and then played a major role in helping the colonies win their independence from Great Britain. He was a scientist and inventor as well as a political leader.

**George Washington** (1732–1799) led American forces during the Revolutionary War and was the unanimous choice to be the first president of the United States.

**Patrick Henry** (1736–1799) spoke out strongly against British taxes and for American independence. He led the battle in Virginia against ratifying the Constitution.

Patrick Henry

**John Jay** (1745–1829) helped write *The Federalist Papers* and was the first chief justice of the U.S. Supreme Court.

**Daniel Shays** (ca. 1747–1825) led protests in Massachusetts against high taxes. Those protests fueled the call to change the U.S. government.

**James Madison** (1751–1836) has been called the Father of the Constitution, as he suggested many of the ideas that became part of it. He also wrote most of the amendments that formed the Bill of Rights. He was the fourth president of the United States.

James Madison

**Gouverneur Morris** (1752–1816) helped write the final draft of the Constitution and was a devoted Federalist.

**Edmund Randolph** (1753–1813) proposed the Virginia Plan, which became the basis for much of the Constitution.

**Alexander Hamilton** (ca. 1755–1804) was General George Washington's top aide during the Revolutionary War and then became a leader in the effort to create a stronger national government. He was killed in a duel with Vice President Aaron Burr.

**Abraham Lincoln** (1809–1865) was the 16th president of the United States, whose election helped spark the Civil War. He opposed the expansion of slavery into the American western territories.

# TIMELINE

| 1775 | 1776 | 1781 | 1783 |
|------|------|------|------|
| The American Revolutionary War begins. | The Americans declare their independence from Great Britain. | U.S. forces win a major victory at Yorktown, Virginia. | The United States gains its independence. |

| 1791 | 1794 | 1804 | 1865–1870 |
|------|------|------|-----------|
| The first 10 amendments are added to the Constitution. | The 11th Amendment is ratified. | The 12th Amendment is ratified. | The states ratify three amendments addressing the end of slavery. |

## 1786

Massachusetts farmers protest taxes in their state, leading to Shays's Rebellion; five states send delegates to the Annapolis Convention to discuss changing the Articles of Confederation.

## 1787

The delegates at the Philadelphia convention write the Constitution.

## 1788

The Constitution is ratified by the states.

## 1789

George Washington is elected the first president of the United States; Congress sends the Bill of Rights to the states for ratification.

## 1920

The 19th Amendment gives women the right to vote.

## 1964

The 24th Amendment forbids states from collecting a poll tax.

## 1971

The 26th Amendment lowers the voting age to 18.

## 1992

The 27th Amendment limits when Congress can give itself pay raises.

# LIVING HISTORY

Primary sources provide firsthand evidence about a topic. Witnesses to a historical event create primary sources. They include autobiographies, newspaper reports of the time, oral histories, photographs, and memoirs. A secondary source analyzes primary sources, and is one step or more removed from the event. Secondary sources include textbooks, encyclopedias, and commentaries.

**The Bill of Rights** To view a copy of the original 12-amendment Bill of Rights, go to *www.archives.gov/legislative/features/bor/*

**George Washington's Diaries** Washington's diaries are kept at the Library of Congress in Washington, D.C., which holds about 144 million items relating to U.S. and world history, ranging from rare books to photos to musical recordings. To see the diaries, go to *http://memory.loc.gov/ammem/gwhtml/gwintro.html*

**Political Victory Banner** To view the victory banner created to celebrate the presidential election of Thomas Jefferson in 1800, go to *www.history.org/history/teaching/enewsletter/volume7/oct08/primsource.cfm*

**The Preamble to the U.S. Constitution** An original copy of the Constitution is kept at the National Archives in Washington, D.C., along with the Declaration of Independence and the Bill of Rights. To see the original Constitution, go to *www.archives.gov/global-pages/larger-image.html?i=/historical-docs/doc-content/images/constitution-l.jpg&c=/historical-docs/doc-content/images/constitution.caption.html*

# RESOURCES

## Books

Bozonelis, Helen Koutras. *A Look at the Nineteenth Amendment: Women Win the Right to Vote*. Berkeley Heights, NJ: Enslow Publishers, 2009.

Burgan, Michael. *The Reconstruction Amendments*. Minneapolis: Compass Point Books, 2006.

Fradin, Dennis. *The U.S. Constitution*. New York: Marshall Cavendish Books, 2007.

Gaines, Ann. *James Madison: Our Fourth President*. Mankato, MN: Child's World, 2009.

Hubbard-Brown, Janet. *How the Constitution Was Created*. New York: Chelsea House, 2007.

Rebman, Renee C. *The Articles of Confederation*. Minneapolis: Compass Point Books, 2006.

Roberts, Russell. *The Life and Times of Alexander Hamilton*. Hockessin, DE: Mitchell Lane Publishers, 2007.

Taylor-Butler, Christine. *The Bill of Rights*. New York: Children's Press, 2008.

## Web Sites

### Charters of Freedom
*www.archives.gov/exhibits/charters*
This online exhibit from the National Archives looks at the Constitution and the Bill of Rights, along with the Declaration of Independence.

### Making of the Constitution
*www.montpelier.org/explore/james_madison/making_constitution.php*
This Web site explores the life and home of James Madison, and this page looks at his role in creating the Constitution and the Bill of Rights.

# GLOSSARY

**amendments** (uh-MEND-muhnts) changes that are made to a law or a legal document

**commerce** (KOM-urss) the buying and selling of goods; business dealings

**compromise** (KOM-pruh-mize) an agreement between two sides that requires each to give up something that it wants

**constitutional** (kahn-sti-TOO-shuh-nuhl) referring to whether a law or action is allowed under a constitution

**debt** (DET) money or something else that someone owes

**delegates** (DEL-i-gitz) representatives to a convention or congress

**executive** (eg-ZEK-yuh-tiv) the part of government that carries out laws, or the person in charge of that department

**federal** (FED-ur-uhl) referring to a system of government that balances power between states and the national government, or another name for the national government

**judicial** (joo-DISH-uhl) relating to the court system

**legislative** (LEJ-iss-lay-tiv) relating to the branch of government that makes laws

**ratify** (RAT-uh-fye) to approve, such as a legal document

**sovereignty** (SOV-ruhn-tee) the supreme power to rule

**unanimously** (yoo-NAN-uh-muhss-lee) with everyone in agreement

**Union** (YOON-yuhn) another name for the United States, or the name for the Northern states during the Civil War

# INDEX

Page numbers in *italics* indicate illustrations.

## ABOUT THE AUTHOR

**Michael Burgan** has written more than 250 books for children and young adults, including both fiction and nonfiction. He specializes in U.S. history and has written many books on colonial America, the American Revolution, and the founding of the nation. He graduated from the University of Connecticut with a degree in history and has won several awards for his work.